# Carrie's War

## About the book

Evacuated from London to Wales during the Second World War, Carrie Willow and her brother Nick are lodged with the strict and miserly village grocer, Mr Evans. This, then, is a novel about children deprived of their parents; but it's also about adults deprived of children. These two themes are almost relentless: Carrie and Nick are metaphorically orphaned by the war; Evans is an orphan (and a widower); Albert Sandwich is an orphan, as are Auntie Lou and Mister Johnny; Dilys Gotobed has no children, nor has Hepzibah.

Separation from parents – even by the nightmare of war – is also a liberation from authority. This is a recurring concept in classic children's literature, one that connects *Carrie's War* to *Little Women*, *Peter Pan* and *The Indian in the Cupboard*, and to films like *ET*, in which children are forced by circumstances to adopt adult responsibilities, and make adult decisions, without the guidance of parents. This, of course, is a possibility both delicious and terrifying. Young Carrie, deeply considerate of other people's feelings, nevertheless makes terrible misjudgements, which hurt her for the rest of her life.

*Carrie's War* was first published over 30 years ago and has never been out of print. The latest BBC adaptation, for Christmas 2003, is now available on DVD. The book owes its classic status not only to the excellence of Bawden's narrative writing, but also to the richness of its characterisation. Evans, for example, is a pathetic ogre of Dickensian complexity. In addition, the structure of the book is beautiful. It's a flashback narrative within a modern time-frame; the opening and closing chapters form a 'mini-novel' which leaves us, tantalisingly, with the possibility of hope and the healing of old wounds. It's not until the very last sentence that Bawden throws us the lifeline of hope and redemption. This is a complex novel which can sustain several readings and reinterpretations.

## About the author

Nina Bawden was born in 1925. She has written over 40 books for both children and adults. During World War II, Nina was evacuated from London to a mining village in Wales, just like the children in *Carrie's War*. Two of her great strengths as a writer are an ability to create characters that are both vivid and complex, and a readiness to write about real issues in a way that is absolutely serious while not at all ponderous. She has a keen awareness of the frustrations of childhood: children, she once observed, are 'a kind of subject race, always at the mercy of adults who mostly run their lives for them.' Or, as Albert complains in *Carrie's War*, 'It's a fearful handicap being a child. You have to stand there and watch, you can never make anything happen.'

Nina Bawden's autobiography, *In My Own Time*, was published in 1995 by Virago.

*Nina Bawden photograph ©Mark Gerson*

> **Facts and figures**
> First published by Puffin Books in 1974
> Adapted by Robert Staunton as a playscript, Oxford University Press 1997
> Adapted for television in 1974 and 2003 (DVD released 2004)
> Audio cassette: Cover to Cover 1996
> Winner of the Phoenix Award 1993

# Guided reading

## Chapter 1

Read and review Chapter 1, which bristles with hooks to snag the reader's interest. What questions does it leave hanging? What is the key mystery here? (Carrie's complicated, mysterious feelings – needing to be there, but sad and afraid at the same time.) What mood is established by Carrie's dream on the first page? Later, she says she was so happy here; is that what her dream and behaviour suggest? Do we suspect Carrie's secret is a 'dark' one? (Look again at the paragraph beginning 'She spoke as if she should have known…' on page 9.)

Ask the children to read ahead Chapters 2 and 3 before the next session.

## Chapter 2

Beginning Chapter 2, we realise that Chapter 1 was a sort of prologue. (It turns out to be much more than that later.) Ensure that the children have grasped the time shift, and have some understanding of the evacuation. Are Carrie's feelings for Nick 'simple'? (No: she loves him, but he is greedy and troublesome; she's burdened by her responsibility for him. Carrie's emotional complexity becomes increasingly significant as the novel progresses.)

How does Nina Bawden build up our expectations of Mr Evans? What does her description of his home tell us about him? How does she create tension? (Through Miss Evans's anxiety.)

## Chapter 3

Read the first three pages of Chapter 3. How does Nina Bawden undermine Mr Evans's fearsomeness? (Nose hair and loose dentures can be comical and tend to encourage disrespect. In these pages, how many references to teeth, mouths and similar can the children spot, and how do they add to Evans's character?) What does Evans's speech tell us about him? (It's full of clichés, suggesting he has difficulty expressing original or personal thoughts.) His speech and behaviour also tell us that he is awkward and ill at ease.

Discuss Mrs Willow's visit. Can the children see that she is desperate to believe that everything is okay? What words can the children offer to describe Evans's behaviour? (Dishonest? Slimy?)

What surprising qualities does Nick show in these chapters? (Bravery and quick-wittedness.) At the end of Chapter 3, do Nick's words come as a surprise? Does Carrie feel the same as Nick? Help the children to recognise that Carrie is always anxious about how other people feel.

Ask the children to read the next two chapters before the next session.

## Chapters 4 and 5

Chapters 4 and 5 complete the 'building up' part of the novel, with the key characters, the skull legend and the two main locations introduced. These locations – Evans's shop and Druid's Bottom – will become the focal points of the novel's dramatic conflict; they represent two opposing ways of life. Ask the children to suggest words to characterise each. Neither place is what it at first seems: Evans's shop, meant to provide safety and nourishment, is mean and oppressive; Druid's Bottom appears darkly forbidding, but is a place of comfort and generosity. Note that Bawden uses food to symbolise the difference between the two places, and between Evans and Hepzibah.

Read from 'The goose…' (page 48) to '…fetch the goose?' (page 50) and ensure the children understand the history of Evans's estrangement from his sister. Then read Hepzibah's telling of the skull story (from page 66). What does Albert's reaction to it tell us about him? (He is rational and unsentimental.) By the end of Chapter 5, the children should understand that Carrie is the kind of person whose sense of responsibility towards others often overrides her own feelings. Discuss the meaning and significance of 'she had to harden her heart' in the penultimate paragraph.

Ask the children to read Chapters 6, 7 and 8 before the next session.

Read & Respond

## KS2

**SECTION 1**

## Carrie's War
Teachers' notes .......................................... 3

**SECTION 2**

## Guided reading
Teachers' notes .......................................... 4

**SECTION 3**

## Shared reading
Teachers' notes ...........................................
Photocopiable extracts ............................... 8

**SECTION 4**

## Plot, character and setting
Activity notes ......................................... 11
Photocopiable activities ...................... 15

**SECTION 5**

## Talk about it
Activity notes ......................................... 19
Photocopiable activities ...................... 22

**SECTION 6**

## Get writing
Activity notes ......................................... 25
Photocopiable activities ...................... 28

**SECTION 7**

## Assessment
Teachers' notes and activities .............. 31
Photocopiable activity ........................ 32

# Read & Respond

## FOR KS2

**Authors:** Mal Peet and Elspeth Graham

**Editor:** Roanne Charles

**Assistant Editor:** Niamh O'Carroll

**Series Designer:** Anna Oliwa

**Designer:** Helen Taylor

**Cover Image:** Angelo Rinaldi

**Illustrations:** Mark Edwards

Text © 2006 Mal Peet and Elspeth Graham
© 2006 Scholastic Ltd

Designed using Adobe InDesign

Published by Scholastic Ltd, Villiers House,
Clarendon Avenue, Leamington Spa,
Warwickshire CV32 5PR

www.scholastic.co.uk

Printed by Bell & Bain
2 3 4 5 6 7 8 9     7 8 9 0 1 2 3 4 5

British Library Cataloguing-in-Publication Data
A catalogue record for this book is available from the British
Library.

ISBN 0-439-96582-9    ISBN 978-0439-96582-8

### Acknowledgements
**Artists Partners on behalf of Mark Edwards** for the reuse of
illustrations from *Scholastic Literacy Centre: Blue Fiction Classics*
© 2003, Mark Edwards (2003, Scholastic Limited). **Penguin
Group (UK)** for the use of extracts from *Carrie's War* by Nina
Bawden © 1974, Nina Bawden (1974, Puffin). **Robert Staunton**
for the use of an extract from *Carrie's War: Oxford Playscript*
by Robert Staunton © 1997 Robert Staunton (1997, Oxford
University Press).

# Chapters 6, 7 and 8

Establish what has been learned so far about Carrie's personality. Have the children noticed that her instinct is always to ease situations and say what people want to hear, although that might involve betraying her own feelings? Carrie does this at the beginning of Chapter 6. What is the consequence? (The row with Nick – he loses some respect for her here.)

After the episode at Druid's Bottom, Carrie is very troubled (the last two pages of Chapter 6). Note that she is increasingly caught between two camps and, characteristically, wants to do what's right for both.

In Chapter 7 comes the pivotal event: Mrs Gotobed's conversation with Carrie. Carrie doesn't yet understand it, but does the group? Does it seem right that such an important message of reconciliation should be made Carrie's responsibility?

How has Nick changed by the end of Chapter 7? Look at the intelligent things he says on the last page of the chapter, and consider his relationship with Mister Johnny: Nick is much more sensitive and understanding than he first seemed and is in some ways more grown up than his elder sister.

At the beginning of Chapter 8, we get more insight into Evans's character from Hepzibah, who may seem a surprising source. Here, Bawden persuades us to reconsider Evans. Does he still seem the 'ogre' we first met?

# Chapter 9

In Chapter 9 Nina Bawden cranks up the tension by suggesting future events that threaten the characters. Albert suggests that Mister Johnny might end up in a 'madhouse' after Mrs Gotobed's death; then Mrs Gotobed arrives at the hayfield in the ball gown, which tells us that she is about to die. Next, Frederick admits that he intends to abandon his father, and finally Mrs Gotobed reminds Carrie that she will soon have to deliver her message to Evans. A great 'wind-up' chapter, and it all seemed so *nice* at first!

# Chapter 10

Read the first five pages of Chapter 10, down to the break '…much of a hurry'. Ensure that the children see that Carrie's understanding of Mrs Gotobed's message is consistent with her character; that she has a stubborn desire to put the kindest interpretation on things and imagine that other people will see things as she does. Who is right: Carrie or Albert? Well, Albert, of course. Draw attention to Albert's mention of a Will; this will prove crucial later on in the story.

Discuss how, in the latter part of Chapter 10 Nina Bawden builds up the dramatic tension by keeping Evans bulging-eyed and silent while Carrie witters on. At the end of this chapter, who seems the wiser: Carrie or Nick?

# Chapter 11

Read the first page and a half of Chapter 11, up to '…Hepzibah's kitchen'. Carrie's anxieties begin to overwhelm her here. What do the children make of the odd picture of the box and the dark shape within it? Is it the box with the skull? It could be; but perhaps Carrie remembers the Greek myth of Pandora's Box, which contained all the evils of the world; when Pandora opened the box, they flew out, leaving only hope inside. Why might Carrie think of herself as like Pandora? Is she perhaps *understanding* her feelings? Is she beginning to realise that by trying to be nice to everybody she has actually spoiled things?

# Chapter 12

At the beginning of Chapter 12, what new aspects of Evans's character emerge? (His scrupulous fairness, even occasional kindness.) What do we learn about Albert in this chapter? (Despite his intelligence, he feels impotent because he's a child; that he can be critical of himself as well as others.)

Ask the group to read Chapters 13 and 14 before the next session.

# Guided reading

## Chapters 13 and 14

These two chapters are an emotional roller-coaster ride, leading to what *appears* to be the novel's tragic climax. The pendulum of Carrie's feelings about Evans swings again. She feels warmer towards him after the picnic and the gifts, yet she is quick to believe, he did, after all, steal the ring and the Will. Why? (Partly because Albert is so sure; but also because Carrie's feelings are so unstable; she lacks the judgement that might balance them.)

Read on from 'Hepzibah said, 'Show me, Carrie love...' (page 166) to '... aren't we Albert?' (page 169). Is Carrie actually thinking, just before she throws the skull, or is this a 'moment of madness'? What does it tell us about her state of mind that she hopes she'll destroy Druid's Bottom to spite Evans? At the end of Chapter 13, is Nick justified in not trusting Carrie to keep a secret?

Read the last conversation between Carrie and Mr Evans early in Chapter 14. With the truth revealed, what, finally, do the group think of Evans? Consider all the people he has lost during his life: is it possible to imagine a future lonelier than his? How might the children describe Carrie's feelings at the end of Chapter 14? Can they see that Carrie's 'curse' is to feel guilty, and responsible, for everything?

Ask the children to read Chapter 15.

## Chapter 15

Does it surprise the children to be 'fast-forwarded' 30 years? Were they expecting to meet the characters from Chapter 1 again? There are surprises, and questions answered, but what is the big question that Nina Bawden leaves hanging over this chapter until the last moment? (It's about Carrie herself – the fact that she still weeps over her experience, and hasn't been able to speak about it or forget it in 30 years tells us that she remains deeply wounded.) Will she at last be healed, somehow? And is she? Does *Carrie's War* have a conventional happy ending? Not quite; but we are left with hope, that last item in Pandora's Box. Are there hints here, as in the first chapter, of a future relationship between Carrie and Albert? Will 'Mr Head' and 'Miss Heart' be united finally? Will Carrie be able, at last, to stop blaming herself?

Discuss the possible meanings of 'War' in the title of the book. Help the children to grasp that Carrie's own war is actually fought within herself.

# Shared reading

## Extract 1

● The first extract is taken from Chapter 2, just after Carrie and Albert meet each other for the first time.

● Here, differences between Carrie and Albert begin to emerge. Albert's reaction to this cattle auction shows strength of character; he is calmly disgusted and marches off. Key words that depict Carrie's feelings are ill, shame and fear; she shows weakness. The most important of these words is shame. Carrie is someone who tends to blame herself for things beyond her control – strongly suggested in Chapter 1.

● 'A nice little girl for Mrs Davies, now.' Why are these words so horrible? Does the group see that the evacuees are being 'shopped for', as if they are things?

● What is Carrie really doing when she unfocuses her eyes? (Hiding from what she doesn't want to see or be part of.) Nonetheless she co-operates: 'Why don't you smile and look nice?' she says to Nick. Note the difference between this frightened, passive reaction and Albert's open defiance.

● Carrie blames Nick for her anxiety and fear. Why is this unfair? Where should she direct her anger, really?

## Extract 2

● Extract 2 is from the very beginning of Chapter 3, where we meet Samuel Evans.

● From a dictionary, children will discover that an ogre is a man-eating monster. With which of Evans's features does this connect, ironically? (His false teeth.)

● Discuss the phrase 'Councillor Samuel Isaac Evans was a bully'. It's a flat, blunt statement, as if to say, 'and that's all.' His full name is given, as if being read out in court. Also note his Old Testament names, which suggest a religious upbringing.

● Who does he bully, and what does this tell us? Which phrase sums up and condemns bullies? ('…if he had thought they were frightened of him').

● This passage tells us a good deal about Nick: in the previous chapter he seemed greedy and feeble; here he shows intelligence and bravery.

● 'A bit of sugar on the pill' is the first of Evans's many clichés. What does this one tell us about his attitude to Carrie and Nick's arrival in his house? (See also Guided reading, page 4, and 'The wit and wisdom of Mr Evans' on page 11.)

## Extract 3

● Extract 3 is from Chapter 14, the penultimate chapter of the novel.

● Does the group understand the 'sail' metaphor in the first sentence? Explore the meaning of 'becalmed'.

● We see Evans the bully crushed and alone. How are we expected to feel? Glad? Satisfied? Ask the group to pick out words and phrases, such as 'the dead fire', 'his bones creaking', 'helplessly', that might make us more sympathetic.

● The way both Carrie and Evans speak here is interesting. It shows a major shift in their relationship. It's very different from the way they communicate at the beginning of the novel. Notice that they both use incomplete, informal, sentences. It's surprising that Carrie says, 'Late you mean, don't you?' and 'You been up all night?' Does it show disrespect, indifference, anger, or perhaps some sort of affection, even intimacy?

● Throughout the novel, food is used symbolically. Discuss the significance of Evans's breakfast menu. What does it tell us about how he has changed?

# Extract 1

*Chapter 2 (pages 19 and 20)*

Carrie looked round, bewildered, and saw Albert Sandwich. She whispered, 'What's happening?' and he said, 'A kind of cattle auction, it seems.'

He sounded calmly disgusted. He gave Carrie her suitcase, then marched to the end of the hall, sat down on his own, and took a book out of his pocket.

Carrie wished she could do that. Sit down and read as if nothing else mattered. But she had already begun to feel ill with shame at the fear that no one would choose her, the way she always felt when they picked teams at school. Suppose she was left to the last! She dragged Nick into the line of waiting children and stood, eyes to the ground, hardly daring to breathe. When someone called out, 'A nice little girl for Mrs Davies, now,' she felt she would suffocate. She looked up but unfocused her eyes so that passing faces blurred and swam in front of her.

Nick's hand tightened in hers. She looked at his white face and the traces of sick round his mouth and wanted to shake him. No one would take home a boy who looked like that, so pale and delicate. They would think he was bound to get ill and be a trouble to them. She said in a low, fierce voice, 'Why don't you smile and look nice,' and he blinked with surprise, looking so small and so sweet that she softened. She said, 'Oh, it's all right, I'm not cross, I won't leave you.'

# Extract 2

*Chapter 3 (pages 30 and 31)*

He wasn't an Ogre, of course. Just a tall, thin, cross man with a loud voice, pale, staring, pop-eyes, and tufts of spiky hair sticking out from each nostril.

Councillor Samuel Isaac Evans was a bully. He bullied his sister. He even bullied the women who came into his shop, selling them things they didn't really want to buy and refusing to stock things that they did. 'Take it or leave it,' he'd say. 'Don't you know there's a war on?'

He would have bullied the children if he had thought they were frightened of him. But although Carrie was a little frightened, she didn't show it, and Nick wasn't frightened at all. He was frightened of Ogres and spiders and crabs and cold water and the dentist and dark nights, but he wasn't often frightened of people. Perhaps this was only because he had never had reason to be until he met Mr Evans, but he wasn't afraid of him, even after that first, dreadful night, because Mr Evans had false teeth that clicked when he talked. 'You can't really be scared of someone whose teeth might fall out,' he told Carrie.

The possibility fascinated him from the beginning, from the moment Mr Evans walked into the kitchen while they were having breakfast their first morning and bared those loose teeth in what he probably thought was a smile. It looked to the children more like the kind of grin a tiger might give before it pounced on its prey. They put down their porridge spoons and stood up, politely and meekly.

It seemed to please him. He said, 'You've got a few manners I see. That's something! That's a bit of sugar on the pill!'

# Extract 3

*Chapter 14 (pages 174 and 175)*

A great wind of rage seemed to blow her along the passage, flung the doors open and then dropped her, becalmed, just inside it.

She breathed hard but said nothing. Mr Evans was sitting there, staring at the dead fire, the poker in his hand. He looked up and saw her and said, in a puzzled voice, 'Bit early, isn't it?'

She said, 'Late you mean, don't you?' and looked at the clock on the mantelpiece. It was half past five in the morning.

Mr Evans said, 'I was just going to wake you. Train goes at seven.' He stood up, his bones creaking, and went to the kitchen window to take the blackout frame down. Light poured in and the sound of birds singing.

Carrie said, 'You been up all night?'

He nodded. He took the kettle from its hook above the fire and filled it at the sink. He hung it back in its place, then knelt to put screwed-up newspaper and kindling in the grate. When it flared up he put the coal on, small lump by small lump as Auntie Lou always did and as Carrie watched him, doing Auntie Lou's job, all the anger went out of her.

He said, 'Soon get it going. Cup of tea, bit of breakfast. Bacon, I thought. Fried bread and tomatoes. Something hot to set you up for the journey.'

Carrie said, in a small voice, 'Not for Nick. The grease might upset him. He gets sick on trains.'

'Porridge, then.' He looked round, rather helplessly.

SCHOLASTIC
www.scholastic.co.uk

READ & RESPOND: Activities based on Carrie's War

# Plot, character and setting

## Information and enigmas

> **Objective:** To develop an active attitude towards reading, seeking answers and anticipating events.
> **What you need:** Photocopiable page 15, copies of *Carrie's War*, writing materials.

### What to do

● Run this activity after Chapter 1 and before Chapter 2. The children could work individually or in pairs.

● Re-read Chapter 1, which is full of hints and mysteries. A troubling atmosphere of dereliction and sadness is established. Nina Bawden does give us a lot of information and clues as to what happened to Carrie, but she also leaves lots of unanswered questions.

● Ask the children to use photocopiable page 15 to summarise the information given in Chapter 1 about Carrie, and about Druid's Bottom.

● Next, ask the children to consider the information that Nina Bawden withholds.

What do we not yet know about Carrie and Druid's Bottom? For example, why does Carrie dream about running away? Why did she go there? Why is Druid's Bottom a ruin? Ask the children to summarise this missing information on the sheet.

● The children can then guess how the story will develop. Ideally, they will realise that there is a connection between Carrie's sense of guilt and the ruined state of Druid's Bottom.

> **Differentiation**
> **For older/more able children:** Review these story predictions in later reading. Were they good ones? Do the children want to change their predictions in the light of new information?
> **For younger/less able children:** Provide the children with particular references in the text to concentrate on. For example, in the first paragraph we are told that Druid's Bottom can be reached by a dirt path beside the railway line; we aren't told why Carrie has a scary dream in which she is running away. Discuss together how the story may develop.

## The wit and wisdom of Mr Evans

> **Objective:** To investigate how a character is presented through dialogue.
> **What you need:** Photocopiable page 16, copies of *Carrie's War*, writing materials, a dictionary of commonplace phrases, such as *Brewer's Dictionary of Phrase and Fable* (Cassell), internet access.

### What to do

● Ensure that the children have read Chapter 3.

● Do the children know what a cliché is? (A tired, overused phrase.)

● Re-read Chapter 3, paying particular attention to pages 32 and 42. Pick out clichés that Mr Evans uses, such as 'you've fallen on your feet'; 'mind your Ps and Qs'; 'toe the chalk line'; 'children today don't know they're born'.

● Ask the children to put four of the clichés in the first column on photocopiable page 16. They

are in old-fashioned vocabulary, but provided the children can pick them out, the task is to try to 'explain' them, using the reference sources.

● Finally, in the third column: can the children explain what the phrases tell them about how Mr Evans feels? For example, he says that the children's good manners are 'a bit of sugar on the pill', suggesting that he sees the children as a pill (something nasty) he has to 'swallow' (put up with) but their manners make this task 'sweeter'.

> **Differentiation**
> **For older/more able children:** Ask the children to list clichés and overused phrases that they are familiar with. How might Mr Evans use them? Can the children write some new dialogue for Mr Evans?
> **For younger/less able children:** The children could list clichés that they're familiar with and try to explain what these phrases mean.

# Plot, character and setting

## Druid's Bottom

> **Objective:** To investigate how settings are built up from small details.
> **What you need:** Photocopiable page 17, copies of *Carrie's War*, writing materials.

### What to do
● Druid's Bottom grows increasingly important as one of the novel's two contrasting locations (the other being Evans's house). Druid's Bottom is a place of secrets as well as comfort.
● Tackle this activity after the children have read Chapter 5. Most of the information given about Druid's Bottom and the people who live there may be gleaned from Chapters 4 and 5.
● Give the children copies of photocopiable page 17. Ask them to use the sheet to compare Evans's house with Druid's Bottom, drawing directly on evidence that they find in the text. Encourage the children to notice the smells, the atmosphere, and the food on offer in the two locations.

● Make sure the children understand that they are asked to write in note form when collating information about the two settings.
● Finally, encourage the children to convey as vividly as possible the contrast between the kitchen and library at Druid's Bottom, this time using whole sentences, to express the atmosphere of these rooms.

> **Differentiation**
> **For older/more able children:** Ask the children to use their completed photocopiable sheets as a basis for a letter from Carrie to her mother, describing her first visit to Druid's Bottom. Remind them to include Carrie's feelings about what she experiences.
> **For younger/less able children:** Ask the children to read carefully pages 57 and 58 and pages 61 and 62. Then, working together, encourage the children to come up with descriptions of the kitchen and the library at Druid's Bottom. The children could use their imaginations to add extra details. What colour are the walls? What do the rooms smell like?

## Who's what?

> **Objective:** To investigate the treatment of different characters.
> **What you need:** Photocopiable page 18, copies of *Carrie's War,* writing materials.

### What to do
● A good point to attempt this activity would be after Chapter 8. At this stage, we know – or think we know – a great deal about the main characters. The children should work individually.
● Hand out copies of photocopiable page 18 and ask the children to think about the four characters shown. What have they learned about these characters? They are all quite complicated personalities. They are also very different people; nonetheless they do share some characteristics.
● Ask the children to draw lines to connect the adjectives to the characters. They may attach one of the words to more than one character.

● Some of the adjectives apply to fairly obvious characteristics that the figures display; others require a degree of character analysis or insight. Tell the children to refer to their copies of *Carrie's War,* where necessary, to find particular evidence to justify their decisions.
● Finally, can the children choose four more adjectives of their own and link them to the appropriate characters?

> **Differentiation**
> **For older/more able children:** Ask children to choose one character from their completed photocopiable sheet and to write a fuller character study, making use of the adjectives they have noted down.
> **For younger/less able children:** Children could use all, or just one or two, of the characters on the photocopiable sheet and compile a list of adjectives to describe them. Encourage them to justify their choices by referring to the text.

# Plot, character and setting

## Where there's a Will

> **Objective:** To develop an active attitude towards reading, to understand and make deductions from the text.
> **What you need:** Copies of *Carrie's War,* paper, writing materials.

### What to do
● If the children attempt this activity before Chapter 14, they may not know, although they may have guessed, that Mrs Gotobed's Will doesn't exist. However, both Carrie and Evans believe, at first, that it does. Carrie's naïve belief that Evans will take the same view of the matter as she does, and Evans's enraged response, are pivotal to the novel's development.
● Ask the children to re-read Chapter 10 – this is where the issue peaks.
● Albert believes that Mrs Gotobed has left a Will and tells Carrie what he believes the terms of the Will are (page 128). Can the children summarise in their own words, using evidence from the text, what Carrie thinks about this Will and how she expects Mr Evans to feel about it?
● Is Carrie right in her judgement about how Mr Evans will feel about his sister's Will? Ask the children to summarise in their own words, using evidence from the text, what Mr Evans really does think about the Will.
● Finally, what do the children think about the Will? Is the nature of the Will kind and thoughtful or is it wrong and cruel? Do the children take the same view as Carrie? Or as Mr Evans? Encourage the children to write a couple of sentences expressing their own point of view.

> **Differentiation**
> **For older/more able children:** Encourage the children, in pairs, to debate Mrs Gotobed's odd behaviour. Is she reasonable or unfair? What evidence do the children have for their views?
> **For younger/less able children:** After re-reading Chapter 10, the children should explain in their own words what Carrie and Mr Evans think of the Will.

## Titles, not numbers

> **Objective:** To secure an understanding of the overall sequence of events in *Carrie's War.*
> **What you need:** Copies of *Carrie's War,* paper, writing materials.

### What to do
● This activity should be attempted when the children have completed *Carrie's War.*
● The chapters in *Carrie's War* are given numbers rather than titles. Explain to the children that they are going to be coming up with a title for each chapter.
● Tell them that they will need to scan each chapter quickly to remind themselves of events. Explain that they will need to decide what the key event or theme of each chapter is and then think up an appropriate chapter title that hints at or anticipates this.
● Remind the children that the words and phrases that they use for their chapter titles should be tantalising and exciting, not just a flat statement of what to expect. 'An ogre with false teeth', for example, would be a better title for Chapter 3 than 'We meet Mr Evans'.
● Explain that the best titles will be only one phrase – they may be tempted to come up with lists of what happens in each chapter.
● Compare some chapter titles as a group and discuss which are the best ones and why.

> **Differentiation**
> **For older/more able children:** Using the completed titles as an aid, ask the children to write a synopsis of *Carrie's War* using as few words as possible.
> **For younger/less able children:** Less able children could work as a group each writing titles for one or two chapters, or, working together to come up with chapter titles for the whole book.

# Plot, character and setting

## Passing the time

> **Objective:** To investigate how the passing of time is conveyed to the reader.
> **What you need:** Copies of *Carrie's War,* paper, writing materials.

### What to do
● Children should attempt this activity after reading the whole novel.
● An obvious narrative device used in *Carrie's War* is the flashback: the story within a story told by the adult Carrie. Discuss this technique with the children. Why has Nina Bawden chosen this structure for her novel? What does it provide/add? What would we lose, as readers, if no flashback was included?
● Ask the children to investigate the passing of time within the main narrative. Nina Bawden doesn't use many 'time indicators', such as 'two weeks later' or 'a month went by'. In fact, the first mention of the time of year is not until page 40. However, there are clear time signals throughout the book, for example birthdays, collecting the goose just before Christmas, hay-making and Dilys Gotobed's death. Ask the children to note down as many of these as they can recall or find.
● From those notes, can the children work out how much time passes between Nick and Carrie's arrival in Wales, and their departure in the penultimate chapter?

> **Differentiation**
> **For older/more able children:** Ask children to construct a timeline, marking key events along it.
> **For younger/less able children:** Support children by giving them events to look for, such as Mrs Willow's visit, Carrie's birthday, Mrs Gotobed's death.

## Mr Head and Miss Heart

> **Objective:** To investigate how two of the main characters are presented through examining their relationship with each other.
> **What you need:** Copies of *Carrie's War,* paper, writing materials.

### What to do
● Children should attempt this activity after reaching the end of the book.
● Carrie and Albert are very different characters. As Hepzibah says 'Talk of opposites! Mr Head and Miss Heart…' Ask the children to make statements about them, using the text as evidence. For example:

| Statement | Evidence |
|---|---|
| Albert is rational and unsentimental. | His reaction to the skull story and his view of Mrs Gotobed's impending death. |
| Carrie is pulled in all directions by her need to say what people want to hear. | The interaction with Evans after visiting Hepzibah (Chapter 6). |
| Carrie is not rational. | Throwing the skull in the pond. |

● Ask the children to consider, and include evidence of, the way Carrie and Albert feel about each other at points throughout the novel.
● We are told in the last chapter that Albert is due this weekend. It seems likely that Albert and Carrie are going to meet up 30 years after they last saw each other. Ask the children to imagine the meeting and write the conversation that the two might have. Encourage them to use language appropriate to these characters, and their current age.

> **Differentiation**
> **For older/more able children:** Ask the children to consider whether Carrie and Albert would go on to have a relationship. Are they suited? What may have happened since they last met? Might they stay as friends? Ensure the children give reasons for answers.
> **For younger/less able children:** Work with the children on their character studies. Ask them to back up their ideas with evidence. Discuss the conversation they might have 30 years later.

# Information and enigmas

In Chapter 1 of *Carrie's War*, Nina Bawden gives us a lot of information, but she also leaves many mysteries and unanswered questions. Use this page to summarise what we are told and not told about Carrie and Druid's Bottom, and to guess how the story will develop.

**What we know**

**What we don't know yet**

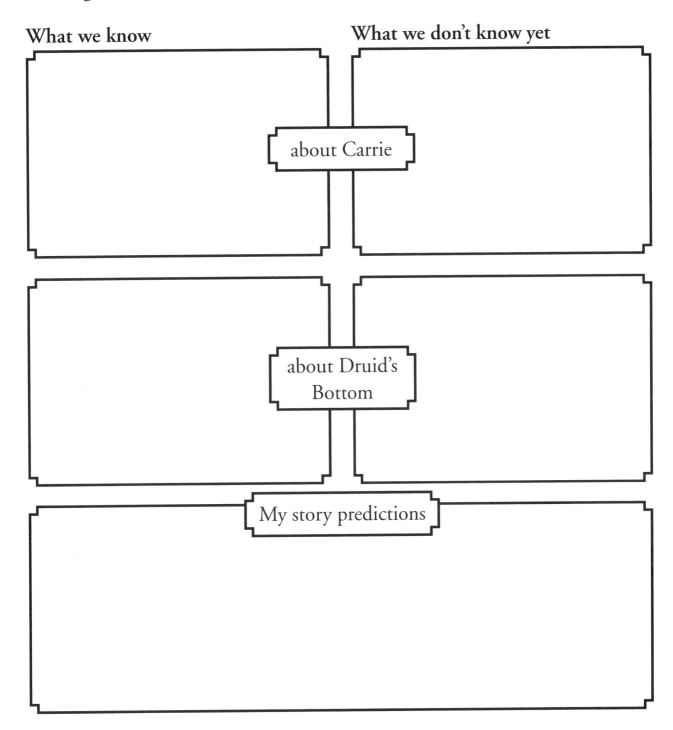

about Carrie

about Druid's Bottom

My story predictions

# Plot, character and setting

# The wit and wisdom of Mr Evans

Mr Evans's speech is littered with clichés. Pick four from Chapter 3, and in the panels below explain what each one means and what it tells us about Mr Evans's attitudes to things.

| Worn-out phrase (cliché) | What it means | What it tells us about Mr Evans's attitudes |
|---|---|---|
| *a bit of sugar on the pill* | *something nice added to something nasty to make it seem better* | *he sees Nick and Carrie as something he has to put up with* |
| | | |
| | | |
| | | |
| | | |

# Druid's Bottom

Compare and contrast Mr Evans's house with
Druid's Bottom. Make notes about the two settings.

**Mr Evans's house**

**Druid's Bottom**

Describe in sentences the atmosphere in:
**the kitchen at Druid's Bottom**

**the library at Druid's Bottom**

# Plot, character and setting

# Who's what?

Draw lines to attach the adjectives to the characters they best describe. Use a different colour line for each character. You might choose to attach some of the words to more than one character. Then try to think of four of your own adjectives to link to the characters.

| | | | |
|---|---|---|---|
| bespectacled | independent | intellectual | friendly |
| unconfident | beautiful | scientific | serious |
| cautious | arachnophobic | competent | kind |
| shy | | | nervous |
| attractive | **Albert** | **Hepzibah** | small |
| greedy | | | insightful |
| truthful | | | generous |
| wise | | | confident |
| maternal | **Nick** | **Auntie Lou** | sceptical |
| clairvoyant | | | tall |

SCHOLASTIC

READ & RESPOND: Activities based on Carrie's War

# Talk about it

## Host families

**Objective:** To constructively discuss and consider a central issue within the novel.
**What you need:** Photocopiable page 22, paper, writing materials.

### What to do

● Explain that thousands of children, like Nick and Carrie, were evacuated to the countryside during World War II. Village communities had to arrange host families to take the children in. In *Carrie's War*, was this was managed well? Could the group do better?
● Organise the children into two groups. One group is to be the village committee; the other children take the roles of host families.
● Cut up photocopiable page 22 and give the cards to the 'host families'.
● Ask the 'village committee' to come up with a list of important questions to ask the host

families. How many spare rooms do they have? Do they have children of their own? What can they offer the evacuees?
● Meanwhile, ask the 'family' children to read their cards and consider their circumstances. How would they feel about accepting evacuees? Would they welcome them or make excuses not to have any?
● Finally, get the committee to ask each host family the list of questions. Decide together who should take in evacuees and how many.

**Differentiation**
**For older/more able children:** Discuss the different needs of the evacuated children and the host families. What are the main problems?
**For younger/less able children:** Work with the children to decide on a list of questions to ask the host families. What are the most important things they need to know?

## A lunchtime drama

**Objective:** To act out a scene from the novel, conveying the unspoken thoughts of the characters.
**What you need:** Copies of *Carrie's War*, a table and five chairs.

### What to do

● Explain to the children that they are going to act out the scene in Chapter 3 in which Mrs Willow has lunch with Mr and Miss Evans.
● Discuss the scene. It is full of awkwardness and things left unsaid. Talk about the unvoiced thoughts of the characters, and how these may be conveyed by expressions and body language.
● There is little dialogue. Ask the children to consider how narrative links might be included. Some possibilities are: the actors improvise extra dialogue; there is a narrator; the actors express themselves soliloquy-style (for example, Carrie explains how tense she is when the subject of biscuits is brought up).

● Organise the children into groups of six or seven – there are five acting roles (Carrie, Nick, Mr Evans, Auntie Lou and Mrs Willow), a director and possibly a narrator. Suggest how they might add narrative links, making sure that different groups try out different techniques.
● Encourage the children to consider and criticise their performances until they feel happy with the scene.

**Differentiation**
**For older/more able children:** Ask the children to write the scene from the point of view of any one of the characters in it. Remind them to concentrate on the feelings and thoughts of that character.
**For younger/less able children:** Read a small part of the scene and discuss what is happening. Ask the children to produce a still image of that part of the scene – as if a photograph had been taken. Then ask the children what their character was thinking at the moment the photograph was taken.

# Talk about it

## In the hot seat

> **Objective:** To investigate character and motivation through question-and-answer role play.
> **What you need:** Copies of *Carrie's War*, paper, writing materials.

### What to do

● Hot-seating is a very simple form of role play, in which one member of the group assumes the role of one of the novel's characters and is 'cross-examined' by the other children.

● This activity can be undertaken at any point during the novel, but is most valuable when there is a significant development or dilemma. It would be a useful exercise at the end of Chapter 10, when Carrie has given Evans his sister's message. Also, Albert could be hot-seated during Chapter 7 and questioned about his feelings towards the other residents of Druid's Bottom.

● Explain hot-seating to the children if they are unfamiliar with the idea, and tell them who they are going to be hot-seating, for example, Carrie in Chapter 3, when her mother comes to visit.

● Ask the children to work in pairs to decide on three questions to ask Carrie. Compile these to create a group list of questions and choose, as a group, which questions are the more interesting.

● It might be a good idea to hot-seat Carrie again as a very last activity, when the children have finished reading and discussing the novel, possibly taking on the role of Carrie yourself. The children's questions will give you a measure of their understanding of the issues in the book as a whole.

> **Differentiation**
> **For older/more able children:** After a hot-seating session the children could use the information to write a journal entry for the particular character about the events that he or she was questioned about. This should give them some clear insights.
> **For younger/less able children:** Hot-seating is a good way to help children understand some of the issues that they may be struggling with.

## Hepzibah and me

> **Objective:** To tell a story orally.
> **What you need:** Photocopiable page 23, copies of *Carrie's War*, writing materials.

### What to do

● This activity should be attempted after the end of Chapter 5.

● Explain to the children that you want them to imagine that they are one of the evacuees in the village hall waiting to be chosen. Hepzibah comes in, chooses them, and takes them home.

● Ask them to think up a story of what happens, concentrating on how they might feel.

● Give the children photocopiable 23 to help them to consider the stages of the incident and what might go through the child's mind. They may wish to make notes on the plan itself or on the back of the sheet, but remind them not to write out the story itself.

● Encourage the children to rehearse their story by telling it a couple of times to a partner.

● Children could then tell their stories aloud to the rest of the class, or to a smaller group of children.

> **Differentiation**
> **For older/more able children:** Ask the children to be critical of their own performance. Was the story convincing? Was it well thought out and well told? Had they rehearsed their telling enough? Do they find it easier to write stories or tell stories? Can they give reasons?
> **For younger/less able children:** The children could concentrate on one part of the photocopiable sheet at a time. First, they should decide which character they are. Then, orally, describe themselves. Only then should they move on to describe where they are and how they feel.

# Talk about it

## Stand up for yourself, Auntie Lou!

> **Objective:** To construct a persuasive argument supporting a point of view.
> **What you need:** Copies of *Carrie's War*, paper, writing materials.

### What to do
● Ensure that the children have read Chapter 7.
● Briefly discuss the statement 'Auntie Lou would be happier if she stood up to her brother'. Explain that this is not a general claim about bullying or gender; it is about two certain people. The children will need to recall what they have learned about these two characters so far.
● Ask the children to prepare their argument for or against the statement, to present to the class. To make a strong and persuasive case they need to be clear, precise and concise (decide on a time limit – one minute is probably about right).

● Tell the children to support their argument with evidence. For example: *Mr Evans looked after Auntie Lou when she was young, so she should live by his rules...* or; *He won't even let her wear lipstick like other women...*
● Ask the children to take turns standing up and giving their arguments.
● Do more children agree than disagree with the statement?

> **Differentiation**
> **For older/more able children:** Ask the children to write a second argument that opposes the first. Are they able to argue both points of view?
> **For younger/less able children:** Initiate a longer discussion. Prompt the children to explain their opinions and decide whether they are for or against the statement. Ask them to write a couple of sentences that put forward their argument.

## The case against Samuel Isaac Evans

> **Objective:** To discuss and judge a central character.
> **What you need:** Photocopiable page 24, copies of *Carrie's War*, writing materials.

### What to do
● Initiate a short discussion about Mr Evans. Ask the children to consider the question 'Is Mr Evans a bad man?' Is he mean, unemotional and cruel? Or fair, lonely and sad?
● Hand out photocopiable page 24. Explain that you are going to put Mr Evans on trial and that you want the children to argue for or against him. Ask the children to prepare an argument, referring to some of the evidence listed at the bottom of the sheet to back up their points.
● Suggest to the children that they can avoid long-winded identification of events by using references such as *At the start of Chapter 3...*
● When the children have prepared their arguments, arrange the prosecution on one side of the room and the defence on the other. Take

on the role of judge and hear all the evidence.
● Ask one child from the prosecution to stand up and provide evidence against Mr Evans, starting with the phrase *Mr Evans is guilty of being mean, unemotional and cruel because...* Next, ask someone from the defence to stand up and give evidence for Mr Evans, countering, *Not guilty! Mr Evans is fair, lonely and sad...* Continue to turn to each side for evidence until no one has any new information to add.
● After hearing all the arguments, make your decision and give your reasons.

> **Differentiation**
> **For older/more able children:** Role play the trial. A child could play Mr Evans, witnesses could be called to give evidence, while others enact the prosecution and defence councils, judge and jury.
> **For younger/less able children:** Involve children in a debate. How do they feel about Mr Evans based on evidence from the novel? Encourage the children to find two good and two bad things to say about him.

# Talk about it

# Host families

| | | |
|---|---|---|
| 70-year-old man. Unmarried. Six bedrooms. | 22-year-old married woman. Pregnant. Husband in the navy. Three bedrooms. | Doctor and wife. She drives ambulance. Both work long hours. Three bedrooms. |
| Married couple. Farmers. Daughter 14, son 12, son 9. Four bedrooms. | Married couple. Retired. Never had children. Three bedrooms. | Young married couple. New baby. Two-bedroomed house. |
| 30-year-old married woman. Husband in RAF. Daughter 6 years old. Two bedrooms. | 34-year-old widow. Husband killed in action. Children: boy 8, girl 10. Two bedrooms. | Vicar and wife. Children: boy 2, boy 5, girl 7, twin boys 9. Five bedrooms. |
| Two elderly sisters. Two-bedroomed house. | Shopkeeper. Lives with old and infirm mother. Three bedrooms. | Married couple in their 80s. Raised a family of six. Three bedrooms. |

■SCHOLASTIC
www.scholastic.co.uk

READ & RESPOND: Activities based on Carrie's War

# Talk about it

# Hepzibah and me

You are one of the evacuated children. You are in the village hall waiting to be chosen. Then Hepzibah comes in and picks you. Use this sheet to plan your story of what happens and how you feel. Make notes to help your planning.

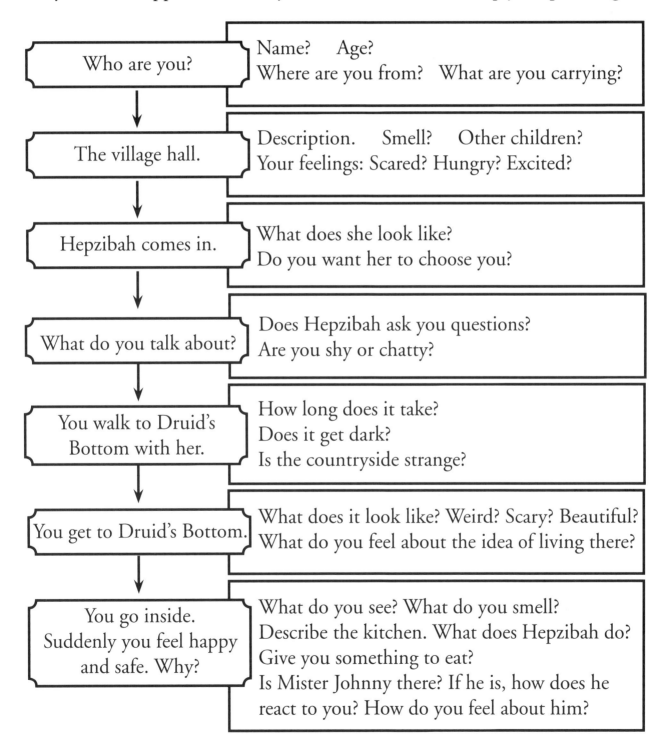

| | |
|---|---|
| Who are you? | Name? Age? Where are you from? What are you carrying? |
| The village hall. | Description. Smell? Other children? Your feelings: Scared? Hungry? Excited? |
| Hepzibah comes in. | What does she look like? Do you want her to choose you? |
| What do you talk about? | Does Hepzibah ask you questions? Are you shy or chatty? |
| You walk to Druid's Bottom with her. | How long does it take? Does it get dark? Is the countryside strange? |
| You get to Druid's Bottom. | What does it look like? Weird? Scary? Beautiful? What do you feel about the idea of living there? |
| You go inside. Suddenly you feel happy and safe. Why? | What do you see? What do you smell? Describe the kitchen. What does Hepzibah do? Give you something to eat? Is Mister Johnny there? If he is, how does he react to you? How do you feel about him? |

# The case against Samuel Isaac Evans

Is Mr Evans a bad man? You be the judge. Use evidence from the box files at the bottom of the page when you make your decision. Make notes below to help you present your evidence.

| Guilty | Judge's verdict | Not guilty |
|---|---|---|

Mr Evans is accused of being mean, unemotional and cruel!

Not guilty! Mr Evans is fair, lonely and sad!

Evidence:
- The way he treats children
- The way he runs his shop
- Nick and the biscuits
- His past life
- The brown envelope

SCHOLASTIC
www.scholastic.co.uk

# Get writing

## A kind of cattle auction

> **Objective:** To rewrite a scene from a different point of view.
> **What you need:** Copies of *Carrie's War*, paper, writing materials.

### What to do

● Ask the children to imagine themselves as a child evacuee in the church hall. Ask them to re-read pages 18 to 21. Explain that their task is to rewrite the scene in the first person, from the point of view of Albert or Nick.

● Prompt the children to find clues in the text about how their character feels. Nick has been sick, he has just been parted from and then reunited with Carrie and he is the youngest and most dependent. Carrie is edgy and rather fed up with Nick, thinking that the state he is in will prevent them from being chosen – how does this make Nick feel? Albert appears to be indifferent to the whole business, but is he, really?

● The children could include the character's thoughts about the others in their writing. Does Nick think that Carrie is being mean, or is he too tired to care? How does Albert feel about Carrie? Does he think her weak and foolish, or is he jealous that she isn't alone like him?

● Suggest the children look for clues in the text. For example, 'Nick clung to Carrie's sleeve, his hand tightened in hers'; 'Carrie dragged Nick into the line'; 'Albert sounded calmly disgusted, he marched across the hall'.

> **Differentiation**
> **For older/more able children:** Ask the children to write from the point of view of Miss Evans. What do the children look like to her? What concerns her – the children, or what her brother will say?
> **For younger/less able children:** Children can assume the characters of Carrie, Nick or Albert and be questioned about their feelings. They can then write the scene from their character's point of view.

## Carrie's two versions of things

> **Objective:** To analyse a character's feelings; to write as that character might in two different situations.
> **What you need:** Copies of *Carrie's War*, paper, writing materials.

### What to do

● Try this activity when the children have read to the end of Chapter 3.

● Point out that there is a time break, an elision, in the middle of Chapter 3 (on page 40). Nick and Carrie have lived with the Evanses for several weeks; their mother has not yet come to visit.

● Ask the children to 'be' Carrie at this point in the story. What is she thinking and feeling? Do they see that Carrie is always anxious about the way that other people feel? At the end of Chapter 3, she is desperate for her mother to be happy. Carrie is afraid of her mother being upset.

● Ask the children to write two things: a postcard from Carrie to her mother, and a page in her secret diary.

● Remind the children that Carrie has a powerful need to say what she thinks people want to hear, though this may not necessarily be the truth. What will be the differences between the two things she writes?

> **Differentiation**
> **For older/more able children:** Children could attempt a longer, sustained piece of writing in the voice and style of *Carrie's War*. Ask them to imagine and detail some events that might take place during this period of time.
> **For younger/less able children:** Discuss how Carrie might feel, being away from her mother for so long, then ask the children to write a page of her diary. Discuss what Carrie might write on a postcard to her mother. Do the children understand that Carrie would keep some things from her mother? Do they understand why?

# Get writing

## Two Carrie Willows on the stage

> **Objective:** To prepare a short section of the story as a script.
> **What you need:** Photocopiable page 28, copies of *Carrie's War*, paper, writing materials.

### What to do

● This activity consolidates the learning in 'Hepzibah and me' on page 20 and challenges them to formalise it in writing.
● Discuss with the children that when a writer has to adapt a novel for the stage (or screen) there is a major problem to deal with – the loss of the narrative voice, and therefore those parts of the novel in which the writer describes things and explains actions, feelings and thoughts.
● Share photocopiable page 28 and explain that this is an extract from a playscript version of *Carrie's War*. The scriptwriter's answer to the loss of narrative voice is interesting, he has two Carries on the stage – the child and the adult.

● Compare the playscript extract with the equivalent text in the novel (pages 53-4). Can they see that in the play, the adult Carrie watches and comments on the action, that she is the narrator?
● Ask the children to continue the playscript in this manner on a further sheet of paper. Remind them that a key issue (plays being shorter than novels) is what to leave out.

> **Differentiation**
> **For older/more able children:** Are the children happy with Robert Staunton's solution to the problem of narrative voice? Ask them to hold discussions in groups to see if they can come up with a preferable solution.
> **For younger/less able children:** Ask children to read both texts, then use the script to act out a performance of the scene. Are the children happy with the performance? Challenge them to improve or extend the script.

## The skull

> **Objective:** To write an imaginative retelling of an extract from the novel.
> **What you need:** Photocopiable page 29, copies of *Carrie's War*, paper, writing materials.

### What to do

● Children could attempt this activity when they have read to the end of Chapter 5. Hepzibah's version of the skull story is in this chapter.
● Read the legend aloud to the children (from page 66 'She sipped her tea…' to page 68 '…no trouble after.').
● Discuss Hepzibah's story. She tells it well – it is clear that she has told it before. She puts dramatic pauses, little teases, into the story, as in 'Nothing happened at all, she waited all day to see…'
● Challenge the children to expand and improve on Hepzibah's version. Hepzibah uses few adjectives and gives us few descriptions; she gives

the little slave no name and no personality. Who was this little African boy? How did he feel so far from home in a strange country? Why did he put that curse on the house?
● Ask the children to take this extra narrative and turn it into a 'real' story. Hand out photocopiable page 29 for the children to use as a planning sheet.

> **Differentiation**
> **For older/more able children:** Ask children to attempt the story from the point of view of the slave boy. They will have to tell part of the story from 'beyond the grave'. Encourage them to think about feelings and motives.
> **For younger/less able children:** Children could first work on a brief character study of the slave. What does he look like? What kind of boy is he? Ask the children to use this character study to help them with a retelling of the skull legend.

# Get writing

## The unseen scene

**Objective:** To imagine a scene not described in the novel and write a script based on it.
**What you need:** Photocopiable page 30, copies of *Carrie's War*, paper, writing materials.

### What to do
● Evans's visit to Druid's Bottom and his confrontation with Hepzibah – one of the crucial events of the novel – takes place 'offstage'. Some information about the visit emerges in Chapter 11. Ask the children to read it again and glean what they can.
● Explain to the children that they are going to create this scene in the form of a playscript. They could work individually, in pairs, or in small groups.
● Give out photocopiable page 30, enlarged to A3 size. First, the children need to note down some rough ideas. As they work, ask the children to consider the following:
  ● What clichés is Mr Evans likely to use in this situation?
  ● How and where do the characters move?
  ● If Albert speaks, what tone of voice might he use? (Angry? Sarcastic?)
  ● How might Mister Johnny react to Evans's visit?
  ● Does the scene need a narrator?
● Finally, the children could write out, or word-process, their final versions onto fresh paper.
● Encourage the children to rehearse their completed scenes, and perform them to the rest of the class.

**Differentiation**
**For older/more able children:** Children could write the next scene, when Mr Evans searches Dilys Gotobed's room. This scene will have little dialogue, although Mr Evans could talk to himself. A lot of thought will have to go into writing stage directions.
**For younger/less able children:** Write the playscript as a shared writing activity to support the children as they deal with all the issues to be considered.

## A different ending

**Objective:** To write an alternative ending for the novel.
**What you need:** Copies of *Carrie's War*, paper, writing materials.

### What to do
● This activity should be attempted when the children have completed the novel.
● Remind the children that the opening and closing chapters frame the main story. Consider the final chapter. If the novel didn't end in this way, with Carrie now 30 years older, how might it end? Discuss some possibilities. Starting points for a final chapter that you might offer are:
  ● Having seen the fire, Carrie and Nick scramble off the train at the next stop and make their way back to Druid's Bottom.
  ● The last chapter takes the form a letter from Albert to Carrie, giving an account of the fire and what happened afterwards.
  ● Mr Evans arrives at the burning house, and dies in the blaze, trying to save something valuable.
● Ask the children to choose one of these, or one of their own, and plan their own final chapter for *Carrie's War*. Then ask them to write it.

**Differentiation**
**For older/more able children:** Ask the children to evaluate their chapter compared to the book's closing chapter. What are its strengths and weaknesses? How would it affect the rest of the story, in hindsight?
**For younger/less able children:** Work closely with the children in the planning stages. Choose the group's favourite ideas and work out the structure for the final chapter together. Support and encourage the children as they write the chapter.

# Two Carrie Willows on the stage

This is a playscript version of a scene on pages 53 to 55 of the novel. In it, the playwright gets round the problem of losing the narrative bits of the novel by having an adult Carrie on stage all the time, explaining and commenting on things. Compare the two texts, and then try to continue the playscript.

**Nick:** *(Wailing)* Carrie, wait for me, wait! Don't leave me Carrie!
*(**Nick** runs forward and holds onto **Carrie**.)*

**Carrie:** *(Jokingly)* I thought it was you leaving me.
*(**Nick** tries to laugh but it turns into a sob. There is a sound like that of deep breathing.)*

**Carrie:** Do be quiet Nick!

**Nick:** Why?

**Carrie:** I don't know.
*(**Carrie** and **Nick** freeze.)*

**Adult Carrie:** Something… something here, something waiting. Deep in the trees or deep in the earth. Not a ghost – nothing so simple. Something old and huge and nameless.

**Nick:** Carrie…

**Carrie:** Listen!

**Nick:** What for?

**Carrie:** Shhh!
*(The two children freeze, listening.)*

**Adult Carrie:** It was as if the earth were turning in its sleep. Or a huge nameless thing were breathing.
*(The breathing stops.)*

**Carrie:** Did you hear?
*(**Nick** cannot reply for his tears.)*

**Carrie:** It's gone now. It wasn't anything.
*(There is the sound of someone running and shouting – it is indistinct and like a gobbling sound.)*

**Nick:** Yes there is! There it is now!

**Carrie:** Run! Don't look back whatever you do!
*(**Carrie** and **Nick** run in panic.)*

**Adult Carrie:** Running, stumbling, slipping, sliding. The gobbling thing following. Calling out after us.

Robert Staunton

# The skull

When Hepzibah tells her version of the legend of the skull she doesn't give much detail. Make notes in the boxes below to help you write your version.

The legend according to Hepzibah:

Who is the little slave boy?

Why did he put such a strange curse on the house?

# The unseen scene

Mr Evans's visit to Druid's Bottom is discussed in Chapter 11, but Nina Bawden doesn't describe it. Try to write the 'missing' scene as part of a play. It might start like this:

---

SCENE: The kitchen at Druid's Bottom. **Hepzibah** is at the table making lunch. **Albert** is sitting near the stove, reading. The door opens.
**Mr Evans** walks in without knocking.
He and **Hepzibah** stare silently at each other for a few moments.

HEPZIBAH: (*Softly*) I'm terribly sorry about your sister, Mr Evans.

EVANS: Oh yes, I dare say you are.
She's been your meal ticket for quite a while, hasn't she?

HEPZIBAH:

---

| Who is there when Mr Evans arrives at Druid's Bottom? (Hepzibah? Albert? Mr Johnny?) | What are they doing? | Do they all speak? |
|---|---|---|
|  |  |  |

# Assessment

## Assessment advice

Nina Bawden deals with tough themes in both her young and adult fiction: 'emotions, motives and the difficulties of being honest with oneself, the gulf between what people say and what they really mean.'

The main narrative of *Carrie's War* is tautly stretched between opposing poles: heart (Carrie) versus head (Albert); uptight meanness (Evans and his home) versus loving generosity (Hepzibah and Druid's Bottom); strictness and the need for hard work (Evans) versus wealth and decadence (Dilys Gotobed). Between these polarities, Carrie, with her desperate need to be fair to everyone, and be approved of by everyone, is torn apart.

Understanding Carrie's nature is key to understanding the issues raised in the book as a whole. To get a measure of the children's understanding of the book, hot-seat Carrie as an assessment activity. The questions that the children ask will show their grasp of the motives and emotions threaded through *Carrie's War*. It is perhaps a good idea, for this purpose, to take on the role of Carrie yourself.

## How Carrie gets it wrong

> **Assessment focus:** To recall the main events of *Carrie's War* and to show an understanding of the central character's thinking.
> **What you need:** Photocopiable page 32, copies of *Carrie's War* (optional), writing materials.

### What to do

● Ruled by her heart rather than her head, Carrie comes to the wrong conclusion about three separate items in the story. These are shown on photocopiable page 32, 'How Carrie gets it wrong'. Hand out individual copies of this page. Ask the children to use the page to summarise Carrie's ideas and assumptions about these events in the story in the left-hand boxes. Next ask them to explain the reality of the events in the right-hand boxes.

● Answers should be along the following lines:

● **Mrs Gotobed's message:** Carrie thinks Evans will be delighted to learn that his sister remained fond of him; and that the contents of her Will were not written to spite him, but to 'do the right thing'. (See the first four pages of Chapter 10.) In fact, Evans is enraged, believing Hepzibah has 'bewitched' his sister and deprived him of his inheritance.

● **The brown envelope:** Carrie believes Albert – that the envelope contains the Will, which Evans has stolen to swindle Hepzibah and Mr Johnny. In fact, touchingly, it contains a photograph of Evans and Dilys as children.

● **The ring:** Carrie believes Albert again – that Evans has 'pinched' it. In fact, Evans had bought it for his sister many years ago, and she had returned it to him when she died.

# How Carrie gets it wrong

Carrie comes to wrong conclusions about the three things on this page: the message Mrs Gotobed gives her for Mr Evans, the missing envelope and Mrs Gotobed's ring. Write what Carrie believes about each of these in the left-hand panels; in the right-hand ones write what turns out to be the truth.

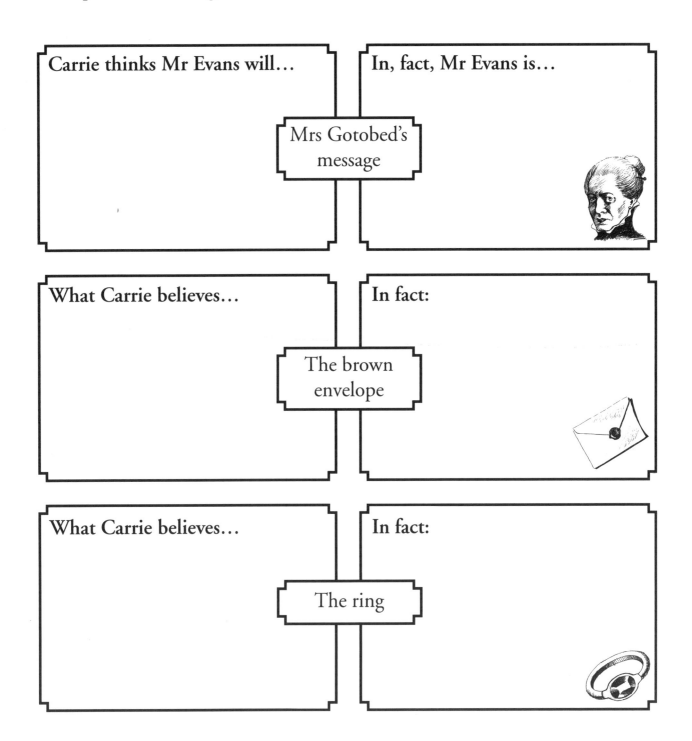

Carrie thinks Mr Evans will…

In, fact, Mr Evans is…

Mrs Gotobed's message

What Carrie believes…

In fact:

The brown envelope

What Carrie believes…

In fact:

The ring